Church of the Small Things

STUDY GUIDE

Other Books by Melanie Shankle

Church of the Small Things

Sparkly Green Earrings

The Antelope in the Living Room

Nobody's Cuter than You

Church of the Small Things

Making a Difference Right Where You Are

STUDY GUIDE

SIX SESSIONS

Melanie Shankle

With Karen Lee-Thorp

ZONDERVAN®

ZONDERVAN

Church of the Small Things Study Guide
Copyright © 2017 by Melanie Shankle

This title is also available as a Zondervan ebook.

Requests for information should be addressed to:
Zondervan, 3900 Sparks Dr., SE, Grand Rapids, MI 49546

ISBN 978-0-310-08134-0

Cover design: Curt Diepenhorst
Cover illustration: Heather Gauthier
Interior design: Kait Lamphere
Interior imagery: © Sociologas/Shutterstock, © Digiselector/Shutterstock, © The_Pixel/Shutterstock

First Printing August 2017 / Printed in the United States of America

Contents

Read This First

When I was growing up, my grandparents were fixtures in my life. My mom's parents, Nanny and Big Bob, lived in the same town with us for many years. Big Bob was an appliance repairman and a man of little speech and much listening. When the females in the family gathered at his house to chatter, he would retire to the next room but tune in to every word that reflected a need among his granddaughters. Once when I was in college, I confided to Nanny that I was broke and overwhelmed, and the next day Big Bob sent me on my way with $100 in cash. Nanny and Big Bob also had a house by a lake, and our family spent weeks there in the summer catching fish, floating in inner tubes, and visiting the local Walmart. So many small, simple things that added up to a stable life where knew I was loved no matter what.

This study is about the small things that can add up to a life well lived and a legacy worth passing down to your children and grandchildren. Many of us think life is about the big things: the college graduation, the proposal, the wedding, the right number of kids, the kids' achievements. But the substance of a life is found in between those big things as we wash the family's clothes, make tacos, and read a children's book at bedtime. If you feel your life is too small, get ready to think of it in a whole new way. A little attention to the small things in life, including friendships and the parts of you that may feel broken, can make a huge difference in something many of us struggle with: a deep sense of contentment and even joy.

Each time you meet with your group, you'll follow this pattern:

- *Getting Settled.* A short introduction will orient you to the theme of the session. You'll read this aloud.
- *Checking In.* You'll start interacting with an icebreaker question that leads into the video teaching. Beginning in session 2, your check-in time will include an opportunity to talk about what you gained from your reflections on your own between meetings.
- *Video Notes.* This guide contains space for you to take notes as you watch the video.
- *Kicking It Around.* This discussion time after the video is where your real growth will take place.
- *Trying It Out.* Each group meeting ends with an exercise you'll do with one or two partners or on your own to put the week's insights into practice. If you're leading the group, please note that in the Trying It Out exercise for session 4 each person will need a sheet of paper and a pen. Otherwise no extra materials are needed. The Bible passages for the discussion are printed out in this guide.

In between group meetings you'll be able to dig more deeply into the small things of your own life. If you can devote a few hours a week to this solo work, you'll surprise yourself with the benefits. The between-sessions exercises come in three sections: Listen to Your Life (reflecting on your past and present experiences), Listen to the Word (some time in the Bible), and Respond to God (a chance to summarize what you've learned through writing, drawing, or other media).

If you're a discussion leader in your group, watch for the highlighted instructions immediately following each section heading. They will tell you when to read something aloud or how much time to allot for an icebreaker question.

A group of women gathered to share life with each other can be a small thing that offers big rewards. It's essential, though, that you make your group a safe place for participants to share openly. A few simple ground rules can help with that. First and foremost is confidentiality: what is shared in the group stays in the group and is not repeated to anyone outside for any reason. Second, be honest about what you think. Third, listen closely to what others think; don't dominate the discussion. Fourth, say no to the temptation to fix or correct others in the group. You're not there to solve others' problems. If you follow these simple guidelines, you can expect to have a great group experience!

Session One

Being Faithful in the Small Things

Live in me. Make your home in me just as I do in you. . . .
I am the Vine, you are the branches. When you're joined
with me and I with you, the relation intimate and organic,
the harvest is sure to be abundant.

John 15:4–5 MSG

Getting Settled

The following paragraphs will orient you to what's coming in this session. Have a group member read them aloud.

When we read the Bible, we can get the impression that life is all about the big moments when God communicates audibly and dramatically with someone and changes his or her life forever. Like when God told Abraham to leave his country and go to a land that God promised to give to Abraham's descendants. Or when God told Abraham he was going to have a son named Isaac the following year.

What we often fail to notice is the long stretches of time that passed between these big moments. Abraham was seventy-five years old when he finally left his country to go to the Promised Land. Seventy-five! What had his life been about all those years before then? He hadn't been raising a family—he was childless. He had been raising sheep and goats, keeping them from tumbling into ravines or getting eaten by wolves (sheep are stupid and helpless). He had been on the move constantly to find water and grazing land for his herds. He had been doing the small daily things of a herdsman.

Abraham was ninety-nine years old when he got the huge news about Isaac. What went on in his life for twenty-four years between Genesis 12:4 and 17:1? A few big moments, including a really dumb decision to have a child with his wife's maid, but mostly a lot of caring for sheep and goats.

Few of us will have the kind of dramatic moments with God that Abraham had. Instead, we will know God—or fail to notice him—in the mundane work of herding sheep or goats or children or office colleagues.

Our life is full of small moments and small wonders that God is using in such a big way. And I think the small moments in our lives are no less holy than the big moments. Maybe it's the small moments that are even more holy, because those are the million little pieces of our lives that God uses to make a difference right where we are.

—Melanie

In this first session, we're going to think about the small things in our lives that shape the people we are becoming. We're going to look for the small ways we make a difference in others' lives—not despite our daily routine but in the midst of it. We're going on a treasure hunt through our very ordinary lives. Your life matters far more than you think.

Checking In

Give each group member one minute to share an answer to this icebreaker question. Your group leader can go first.

What was one small thing you did today for someone else?

Video Notes

Watch the video teaching segment for session 1. Use the outline below to fill in your thoughts about what you get out of the video.

Round Top, Texas

"There are many of us that are willing to do great things for the Lord, but few of us are willing to do little things." —Dwight L. Moody

The feeding of the five thousand

God's will

The possibilities are endless

Vine and branches

In the grocery store

Kicking It Around

Discuss the following questions in your group. If there are more than twelve of you, consider dividing into smaller groups for discussion. Or select those questions that seem most compelling to you.

   1. Which of Melanie's thoughts from this session's video resonated most with you, and why?

When Jesus looked up and saw a great crowd coming toward him, he said to Philip, "Where shall we buy bread for these people to eat?" He asked this only to test him, for he already had in mind what he was going to do.

Philip answered him, "It would take more than half a year's wages to buy enough bread for each one to have a bite!"

Another of his disciples, Andrew, Simon Peter's brother, spoke up, "Here is a boy with five small barley loaves and two small fish, but how far will they go among so many?"

Jesus said, "Have the people sit down." There was plenty of grass in that place, and they sat down (about five thousand men were there). Jesus then took the loaves, gave thanks, and distributed to those who were seated as much as they wanted. He did the same with the fish.

(John 6:5–11)

2. Think about John 6:5–11. What if the person who packed the boy's lunch never learned that five thousand people were miraculously fed by that lunch? How is this like or unlike the situation you find yourself in most days?

3. Do people tend to thank you for the small things you do during your day? Why do you suppose that's the case? How does that affect you?

We're in God's will when we wake up every day with a willingness to say, "God, I'm going to go where you lead me to go today. What do you have for me today? Where can I be faithful to you today? This family that you've given me, this job that you've given me, this life that you've given me—where can I show up and be faithful today?" It may not be the glamorous thing, but it's the faithful thing.

—Melanie

4. What was the faithful thing for you to do today?

5. What helps you notice and do the faithful thing? What gets in the way?

We can spend so much time wondering and worrying if we're fulfilling God's primary will for our lives. Yet, ultimately, God's will isn't about the things we achieve; it's about the people we become.

—Church of the Small Things, page 12

6. What kind of person do you want to become?

How does someone become that kind of person? What role might small actions play?

Trying It Out

Pair up with a partner. Take five minutes to talk about your day, and let your partner help you see where God was at work in the small things. Then switch and spend five minutes talking about your partner's day. Your leader will keep track of time.

Below are some discussion starters. Use any of them that are helpful.

The main things I remember about my day were _____.

God may have been at work when _____.

One of the challenges I faced today was _____.
God helped me through that by _____.

On Your Own

Session One

If you really want to get somewhere in this study, take some time before the next group session to work through these solo exercises.

Listen to Your Life

"I am the true vine. . . . Remain in me, as I also remain in you. No branch can bear fruit by itself; it must remain in the vine. Neither can you bear fruit unless you remain in me."

(John 15:1, 4)

Think about these John 15 verses. What do you think it means to "remain" in Jesus? (Other translations use the words "abide in" or "live in"—what does that mean?) How do you go about staying connected to the Source that gives you the ability to bear fruit?

Which of these sounds most like you?

- ☐ I try very hard to bear fruit.
- ☐ I try very hard to remain in Jesus and leave the worries about fruit-bearing to him.
- ☐ I'm desperately trying to keep my head above water with all the things I have to do, so I don't try very hard to do either of these things.
- ☐ Something else (describe yourself):

What is something you want to do, or stop doing, in light of what you have learned so far about small things and bearing fruit?

Listen to your life. See it for the fathomless mystery it is. In the boredom and pain of it, no less than in the excitement and gladness: touch, taste, smell your way to the holy and hidden heart of it, because in the last analysis all moments are key moments, and life itself is grace.

—*Frederick Buechner, Now and Then*

Most of us do a lot for other people that we don't think of as "ministry" or "servant-hood." We think of it as mothering or doing the job that pays the mortgage. But we need to become aware of the dignity attached to these things that we do.

Write down ten things you've done this week to make someone else's life better. These can be very small things like washing your children's underwear or creating a clear and accurate spreadsheet or collecting a neighbor's mail while she is out of town.

1. _____
2. _____
3. _____
4. _____
5. _____
6. _____
7. _____
8. _____
9. _____
10. _____

What themes do you see running through these great or small acts of generosity? Maybe your first reaction is, *Oh yeah, isn't it great to be an underpaid (or unpaid) drudge! My life is about as exciting as watching ice cream melt.* Have a laugh or a cry about it. But then cycle back around and think about what you've written. Or maybe your work is highly fulfilling and important, but until now you haven't thought of the things you do as helping other people.

What do you notice? For instance, who do you care for? Do you tend to do these things with an attitude of boredom or frustration or flat-out anger? Or do you do them with some other attitude? Are you aware of any moments of joy in these small things? (If the answer is no, that's fine. This is only session 1!)

Think about one of the actions you've listed above. How did it possibly make a difference in someone's life, even if the person wasn't aware of it or didn't thank you?

Nothing is wasted when we view it through the lens of what God has for us in whatever life brings our way. It's all a part of who we are and who he is making us to be. For some, that may be a public role on a big stage, but for the vast majority of us, it's about being faithful in the small stuff: going to the grocery store, volunteering in our kid's classroom, befriending the new girl, coaching a Little League team, showing up for work every day, being kind to our neighbors.

—Church of the Small Things, page 25

On pages 22–23, create a timeline of your life, from birth until now. Mark it with the big moments like "graduated from high school," "graduated from college," "landed first job doing _____," "got engaged," and so on. (Draw a picture or two if you'd like!) Then see if you can also mark it with at least three moments or stretches of time when you learned something significant that has affected you for good or ill since then.

Describe those three life lessons here, along with the moments or stretches of time that went with them:

Lesson #1

Lesson #2

Lesson #3

> Sometimes we get caught up in thinking that the thing God has for us is something huge but hidden, and we either have to work really hard to figure it all out or wait until he drops that thing in our laps like manna from heaven.
>
> *—Church of the Small Things, page 24*

Which of these are true of you?

- ☐ I have been working really hard to figure out what huge thing God has for me.
- ☐ I have been waiting for God to drop a huge thing (a calling) into my lap.
- ☐ I have a huge calling, and I have been following where it leads.
- ☐ I look for small callings in the daily ordinariness of life.
- ☐ I have been pursuing a huge calling, but it hasn't worked out the way I expected.
- ☐ None of the above.

The Timeline of My Life

The Timeline of My Life

Is there anything more you want to say about your experience of calling or lack thereof?

Listen to the Word

The book of Ruth is four short chapters about two women named Ruth and Naomi. At the beginning of the story, Naomi and her husband leave the Promised Land and move to the neighboring pagan country of Moab because of a famine in their part of Israel (Judah). Leaving the Promised Land shows a lack of faith—it equals saying that the Lord, the God of Israel, won't provide for them in the land he gave them. Sure enough, bad things happen to Naomi in Moab: her husband and both sons die.

Ruth is one of Naomi's Moabite daughters-in-law. Israelites aren't supposed to marry Moabites because of the temptation to worship Moabite gods. Ruth knows nothing about Naomi's God other than what Naomi and her family have told her. She does know that she's likely to be unwelcome back in Judah—a foreigner from a pagan nation.

Over the course of this study guide we will read the book of Ruth to see what it can tell us about living in the Church of the Small Things.

Read Ruth 1.

What does Ruth do in this first chapter?

Would you say what she does is a big thing or a small thing? Why?

What appears to be Ruth's motivation for doing what she does?

Where is God in this story so far? Would you say his role is obvious or hidden in this chapter? Why?

What in this chapter of Ruth is relevant to you as you seek to discern God in the small things of your life?

A life isn't made from one thing, one big moment, or one huge success. It's created moment by moment, often with pieces that don't look like anything beautiful on their own but are the very fabric of who God meant for us to become as we pack lunches, raise kids, love our neighbors, and simply be who he created us to be; nothing more, nothing less.

—Church of the Small Things, page 15

Respond to God

Hopefully, all of this listening has gotten your mind and heart whirring in gear and ready to respond. God wants you to offer to him the honest thoughts and feelings that have arisen in you. See if you can put them into words in a letter to God.

Dear God,

Thank you for the small things in my life. Most specifically, thank you for

I am grateful for these because

What I've learned so far from listening to my life is

I still wonder about

I'm hoping that by the end of this study I will

I also want to tell you that

Much love,

Session Two

Created for a Reason

For we are God's masterpiece. He has created us anew in Christ Jesus, so we can do the good things he planned for us long ago.

Ephesians 2:10 NLT

Getting Settled

The following paragraphs will orient you to what's coming in this session. Have a group member read them aloud.

Pastor Gordon MacDonald recounts an old story about God's calling:

> A young farmer, standing in his field, observes a peculiar cloud formation. The clouds form the letters G, P, and C, and he thinks them a call from God: *Go preach Christ!*
>
> The farmer rushes to the deacons of his church and insists that he has been called to preach. Respectful of his ardor, they invite him to fill the pulpit.
>
> That Sunday, the sermon is long, tedious, virtually incoherent. When it finally ends, the leaders sit in stunned silence. Finally, a wizened deacon mutters to the would-be preacher, "Seems to me the clouds were saying 'Go plant corn.'"[1]

Doesn't discerning the call of God often feel like that? We stare upward and try desperately to read God's message in the clouds, while ignoring what we might learn from the abilities God has equipped us with and the path he already has us on. Our abilities seem so trivial, and the path we're on is so ordinary. Surely, we think, God must have something extraordinary for us to do. Yet what if God is at work through the ordinary things of our daily lives to bring about that unique contribution we're going to make?

How do I achieve my God-given destiny when I'm surrounded by kids and laundry and finals and exams and I'm just trying to figure out what to cook for dinner? Where do I find my significance in all of that?

—*Melanie*

In this session, we'll talk about that sometimes scary, sometimes confusing idea of calling. We'll see that God created each of us unique, and he longs to use us in every ordinary and extraordinary piece of our lives.

Checking In

Give each group member up to two minutes to share answers to these questions. Your group leader can go first.

What is one thing you learned or gained from the On Your Own exercises this past week?

What is one thing you're good at?

Video Notes

Watch the video teaching segment for session 2. Use the outline below to fill in your thoughts about what you get out of the video.

God's workmanship of unique people

Searching for meaning and purpose

How Melanie began to write

David: God sees us even when the world doesn't.

God sometimes teaches us the biggest lessons through obscurity.

A calling from God requires us to wait on his timing.

God's calling often means leaving behind the comfortable and the familiar.

We can't compare our calling to others' callings.

Kicking It Around

Discuss the following questions in your group. If there are more than twelve of you, consider dividing into smaller groups for discussion. Or select those questions that seem most compelling to you.

1. Which of Melanie's thoughts from this session's video resonated most with you, and why?

I think it's so cool to think that before the foundations of the world were even laid, that God had a purpose for us. That he knew he was going to create us uniquely for this time and this generation and this space that we occupy. And it makes me wonder, what does he have for us as we are willing to use our unique gifts to make a difference in the world? When we start to feel like God wants to use us for something, it's usually something we don't have the power to do in our own strength.

—*Melanie*

2. Have you ever felt called to be or do something? If so, what was it? What made you think it was a calling? If not, what do you think about the idea of being called to be or do something?

3. Do you feel significant? If so, what helps you feel that way? If not, what do you think gets in the way?

David became one of Israel's great military leaders. He learned key foundational qualities for this role not in Israel's army but while taking care of his father's sheep, as the youngest son in a large family. Consider these two passages. The first is a passage about David, where he volunteers to fight Goliath, the Philistine giant. The second is a psalm he wrote.

David said to Saul, "Let no one lose heart on account of this Philistine; your servant will go and fight him."

Saul replied, "You are not able to go out against this Philistine and fight him; you are only a young man, and he has been a warrior from his youth."

But David said to Saul, "Your servant has been keeping his father's sheep. When a lion or a bear came and carried off a sheep from the flock, I went after it, struck it and rescued the sheep from its mouth. When it turned on me, I seized it by its hair, struck it and killed it. Your servant has killed both the lion and the bear; this uncircumcised Philistine will be like one of them, because he has defied the armies of the living God. The Lord who rescued me from the paw of the lion and the paw of the bear will rescue me from the hand of this Philistine."

(1 Samuel 17:32–37)

The Lord is my shepherd, I lack nothing.
    He makes me lie down in green pastures,
he leads me beside quiet waters,
    he refreshes my soul.
He guides me along the right paths
    for his name's sake.
Even though I walk
    through the darkest valley,
I will fear no evil,
    for you are with me;
your rod and your staff,
    they comfort me.

(Psalm 23:1–4)

4. From these two passages, what did David learn from his years of tending sheep that would help to equip him to be a leader?

5. What is one lesson you are learning in your current life circumstances that could help to equip you in the next stage of your service to the Lord?

6. Do you feel totally capable of doing what God has given you to do at this stage of your life? If so, what more might God have for you? If not, what is God asking of you that you need him to help you with?

We're like, "I can't do that, I'm so freaked out, that's so beyond me, there's no way I can leave this, because this is so comfortable, it's so familiar, and I know what to expect here." And God is saying, "We're not just going from A to B, there are all these little steps in between that are going to prepare you, and I'm going to make you ready. And when that moment comes when you have to leave the comfortable and familiar behind, we'll see it."

—*Melanie*

7. How do you feel about leaving the comfortable and familiar behind in order to follow God's leading? Why?

Here's the thing. It's easier to sit on your couch than to risk failing. It's easier to sit on your couch than to be out in the world where you're vulnerable and open to being hurt or disappointed. But you know what happens while you sit on your couch in your pajamas playing Candy Crush and watching Tami Taylor? Real pants with buttons and zippers. Also, *life*. Beautiful, gorgeous, fragile, heartbreaking, mind-blowing life. God has a script written for each and every one of us, no matter who we are or what we've done or how ill-equipped for the adventure we feel.

We are all climbing our own versions of Mount Everest and have no idea if our oxygen will last or if an avalanche will come, but God does. We can never underestimate the grace and the strength he will give us for whatever he is calling us to do and whatever challenges we'll face. What he has planned for us is higher and deeper than anything we could ever hope to achieve on our own.

It's too much. It's too much for us to do in our own strength because we will mess it up, but he knows that and uses us anyway. It's never about creating or doing or being something that's perfect. It's not about having all the right answers. It's about being his. It's knowing that he who has called us is faithful.

—Church of the Small Things, pages 146–147

Trying It Out

Pair up with a partner. Take five minutes to brainstorm something you can do in service to God that is outside your comfort zone. If you're having trouble thinking of something, enlist your partner's help. Talk about the restrictions in your life, if you have them, but don't make excuses for doing nothing. After five minutes, switch and help your partner think of something she can do. If you and your partner are friends, you can agree to do something together.

Here are some ideas to get you started:

- Bake cookies for your newest neighbors. Drop by with your contact information, and offer to be helpful to them in any way you can. If you work long hours and don't have time to bake cookies, consider dropping by with a gift card for a favorite local restaurant instead.
- Plant a vegetable or herb garden, starting with even one plant, such as tomatoes or basil. If you already have a garden, offer to help someone else plant one. (You and your partner can decide to work on one together.)
- Offer to drive someone else's child to an afterschool activity.
- Tell someone at work something you like about her.
- Let a neighbor's child come to your home before school because the parents have to leave early for work. Offer to feed the child breakfast and join you in a carpool to school.
- Pick up groceries for a neighbor who has trouble getting out.
- Do chores for a pregnant woman.
- After church, make a point of talking with someone you don't know who appears to be alone.

On Your Own

Session Two

If you really want to get somewhere in this study, take some time before the next group session to work through these solo exercises.

Listen to Your Life

Does anyone dare despise this day of small beginnings?

(Zechariah 4:10 MSG)

As you did in session 1, write down ten things you've done this week to make someone else's life better.

1. _____
2. _____
3. _____
4. _____
5. _____
6. _____
7. _____
8. _____

9. _____

10. _____

Put a check mark beside any of these actions that were outside your comfort zone, that stretched you beyond what you're used to doing or beyond what you can do in your own strength without God's help. Pause to thank God for helping you with all of these actions.

David trusted God to enable him to kill the lion and the bear. He then trusted God to enable him to defeat Goliath. What can you trust God to enable you to do? Make it a goal to increase the number of your out-of-the-comfort-zone actions by two by the time you do the solo exercises for session 3.

Depending on your inborn temperament, venturing outside your comfort zone may be exhilarating or terrifying or no big deal. If it's no big deal, try pushing yourself a little further until you feel it. The intent here is to put yourself in a situation where you know you need God to help you.

If you are at the terrified or otherwise-averse end of the spectrum, it may be helpful to talk with God about what you're feeling. You'll need his help to push through these emotions enough to take action. When you get some experience of stretching outside your comfort zone, you will gradually feel less fear. The fear may not go away, but it will be less debilitating.

Dear God,

When I think about doing things outside my comfort zone I feel

What goes on in my head is

What I want to do is

With your help, what I'm going to do is

Much love,

God teaches us the most important lessons in obscurity. While tending sheep, David learned responsibility, and he learned how big God is. Moses also spent several decades herding sheep in the wilderness, and that taught him humility. He learned to manage his impatience and wait on God's timing instead of rushing in and trying to do something grandiose on his own.

Look back at your list of ten things on pages 39–40. What are you learning about God from activities like these? What are you learning about yourself?

To see how you can make a difference in your world right where you are, think about the circles of people you have contact with: your family, the parents of your children's friends, the parents of the other kids at soccer practice, your parents and their peers, the people who attend your church whom you barely know, your friends, your coworkers, the people who work at your gym.

Make a list of these circles in which you travel. Or if it helps you to picture them better, draw circles and label them.

Is there one circle that God might be inviting you to invest in? Or some individuals whose needs are on your heart? Write down who they are and any needs they might have. If you don't know their needs, make a plan to initiate getting to know them better.

Is there a burden on your heart for any individual or group? What is it?

Do you have a hobby or an ability that you've never thought of as ministry—a craft, music, writing, organizing? What is something you would be willing to put to God's use?

What holds you back? Is it busyness? Feelings of inadequacy? Fear of failure? Write it down. And then tell someone (your spouse, a friend) about what holds you back from investing in your world.

As I listened—really listened—I felt God say to me, "You feel like this is too much because you're trying to figure out how to do it in your own power, and none of this is about you." It took everything in me not to just pull the car over and cry, because that's exactly it. I try so hard to be graceful and compassionate and kind and wise and discerning and loving, but I'm putting myself in charge of the production of all those attributes. And then my selfishness and pride and insecurity all rise to the top instead, and I freak out because I know how lacking I am in basically every category, and then I just want to sit on my couch in my pajamas and watch old episodes of *Friday Night Lights* because it feels safe.

—Church of the Small Things, page 146

Listen to the Word

In session 1, we saw how Ruth took a risk and went back to her mother-in-law's homeland because her mother-in-law needed her. Now we'll begin to find out what happened to Ruth in the fields outside Bethlehem.

It's helpful to know a little about the way a barley harvest worked. In April, when the grain was ripe, a landowner would send his workers into the field to cut down the stalks of barley and gather them into bundles. The cutting was done by hand using sickles. Inevitably, some of the stalks would fall to the ground. An efficient landowner might want his people to go back into the field and gather up all those fallen stalks so he would have 100 percent of the harvest. But the law of Moses said that fallen grain should be left for poor people to glean (Leviticus 19:9–10). This was not a handout; the poor would have to do all the backbreaking work of gathering the barley, and then pounding and threshing it to separate the kernels of grain from the worthless chaff. Still, it was a way of providing labor and food for the most vulnerable members of society.

It's also helpful to know that childless widows were usually among the most vulnerable in ancient Israel. They couldn't hire themselves out as day laborers the way a man could, and they couldn't defend themselves against molestation. Male relatives were supposed to look after the women and girls of the family, but without husbands, brothers, or sons, Ruth and Naomi were in a precarious position.

A person's "guardian-redeemer" (see Ruth 2:20) was a relative responsible to restore her rights.

Read Ruth 2.

What small things does Ruth do in this chapter?

What small things does Boaz do? List as many as you can.

How do these small things add up to a big help for Ruth and Naomi?

What could have happened to Ruth if Boaz had been a different kind of person?

Where is God in this chapter?

What in this chapter of Ruth is relevant to you as you seek to discern God's calling in the small things of your life?

Respond to God

Pull together everything you've been thinking in your group and on your own about God's calling for you. Pray and ask God to show you who you are called to be and what you are called to do at this stage of your life. Then write a paragraph or draw a picture that expresses what you currently think your calling includes. Maybe your sense of calling is a work in progress and not entirely clear yet. That's okay. Describe or depict what you think you know about it at this point. If you just have glimpses, maybe you want to scatter some words and phrases or make a collage of images.

Session Three

A Word Fitly Spoken

A word fitly spoken is like apples of gold in a setting of silver.

Proverbs 25:11 ESV

Getting Settled

The following paragraphs will orient you to what's coming in this session. Have a group member read them aloud.

Words seem like small things, but think of how our lives can be changed by just a handful of words:

> Will you marry me?
> I've never loved you.
> Does this outfit make me look fat? (Kiss that friendship good-bye!)

Seriously, though, it's a challenge to control what comes out of our mouths or what gets typed on our phones and sent off into other people's lives. So much good and so much damage can be done, and yet many of us speak without thinking first or can't remember what we've said even an hour or two ago.

Our words are rarely if ever neutral. Jesus even says, "From the overflow of your heart, your mouth speaks." Think about what's in your heart: it's your dreams and your feelings and your passions and your hopes and your aspirations. And all your deepest darkest things. . . . We live in a society where there have never been so many ways to put our words out there for consumption. . . . How careful we need to be that our words overflow from hearts that are filled with God's love, and his kindness, and the way he would have us treat people.

—Melanie

In this session, you'll have a chance to reflect on what you say and write, and what that reveals about what's going on in your heart. It's truly possible to develop the practice of double-checking before we speak.

Checking In

Give each group member up to two minutes to share answers to these questions. Your group leader can go first.

What is one thing you learned or gained from the On Your Own exercises this past week?

Talkativeness is a part of temperament and isn't in itself a bad thing. How would you rate your tendency to say what's on your mind on a scale of 1 to 5, where 1 = "I'm not much of a talker. I tend to be very slow to say what's on my mind" and 5 = "I'm a talker! I tend to blurt out whatever is on my mind"?

Video Notes

Watch the video teaching segment for session 3. Use the outline below to fill in your thoughts about what you get out of the video.

The power of words

What is the purpose of our words?

The gravity of harmful words

What our words were intended to do

Responding to past and future words that hurt us

Kicking It Around

Discuss the following questions in your group. If there are more than twelve of you, consider dividing into smaller groups for discussion. Or select those questions that seem most compelling to you.

1. Which of Melanie's thoughts from this session's video resonated most with you, and why?

2. What is something you said today that you remember because (a) you wish you hadn't said it, or, (b) you know it was aimed at making life better for someone?

3. If you can't remember anything you said today that was good or bad, why do you suppose that's the case?

May the words of my mouth and the meditation of my heart

    be pleasing in your sight,

    O Lord, my Rock and my Redeemer.

(Psalm 19:14 NIV 1984)

He who guards his lips guards his life,

    but he who speaks rashly will come to ruin.

(Proverbs 13:3 NIV 1984)

The good man brings good things out of the good stored up in his heart, and the evil man brings evil things out of the evil stored up in his heart. For out of the overflow of his heart his mouth speaks.

(Luke 6:45 NIV 1984)

When words are many, sin is not absent,

    but he who holds his tongue is wise.

(Proverbs 10:19 NIV 1984)

Finally, brothers and sisters, whatever is true, whatever is noble, whatever is right, whatever is pure, whatever is lovely, whatever is admirable—if anything is excellent or praiseworthy—think about such things.

(Philippians 4:8)

4. Choose one of the Scripture passages above and talk about why it is especially important for you to keep in mind.

We can't let the rest of our lives be determined by hurtful words that were spoken over us all those years before. So I think if you're like me and you've had words in your life that were said over you that were hurtful, that have made you feel less than, that have made you feel ashamed, that have made you feel like you're broken or damaged beyond repair, that's when we need to ask God to come in, and say, "God I need you to show me who I am in your eyes. Show me my worth and my value and the way you see me and what you've created me for."

—Melanie

5. Have you ever been on the receiving end of hurtful words? If so, how have they affected you?

How could God help you to forgive and get past that memory?

What does it say about us that there are people who are so desperate to hear positive things about themselves that they're going to wear headphones? Maybe we need to have real-life people who will build us up. And we need to be those real-life people, encouraging the people around us, and equipping them, and making them feel known and appreciated.

—Melanie

6. Think about the "I'm enough mirror." Do you have people in your life who build you up? Does it work, or do you tend to deflect good words and believe the negative? Explain.

7. What sorts of things could you say to others that would encourage them and make them feel known and appreciated?

Trying It Out

Gather with a group of three people. Let one person briefly share an area of her life in which she could use encouragement and building up. Then let the other two people put their hands on her and pray words that speak to her need. Aim for encouragement and strengthening rather than advice.

When you've prayed for this person, let the other two in your triad each take a turn at being prayed for.

On Your Own

Session Three

If you really want to get somewhere in this study, take some time before the next group session to work through these solo exercises.

Listen to Your Life

I want my words to be pleasing. I want them to be words that God would have me speak, and I want them to be words of encouragement and life.

—Melanie

Write down ten things you've said (either aloud, in a text, or other written format) this week that you either regret saying or are glad you said. If you can't remember ten things all at once, pay attention to your speech this week and write down what you notice yourself saying.

1. _____
2. _____
3. _____
4. _____
5. _____
6. _____

7. _____

8. _____

9. _____

10. _____

Out of the overflow of the heart, the mouth speaks. What do these words you've written tell you about your heart?

If you're feeling guilty right now because of things you've said that you regret, especially if you have children or coworkers or parents who know exactly how to press your buttons and send you into crazy land, this is a chance to go to God for some much-needed forgiveness and a fresh start. There's no one-time perfect fix for a mouth and heart that go from zero to unglued in a fraction of a second, but if you keep paying attention to what you say and asking God and your family for forgiveness, you will change over time.

So, stand up or kneel or get into whatever posture says you mean business, and pray for forgiveness and a new start. You might say,

Woe to me, God, for I am a person of unclean lips! You know the things I've said don't honor you and build up the people you've entrusted to my care, and I can't change that without your help. Please forgive me. I want to be different. Do I need to ask a person's forgiveness? That will feel awkward, but I'm willing to do whatever I need to do to start again the right way. Please also work in me to be able to think before I speak and to control my temper. Please don't let me harm people with my words. In Jesus' name, Amen.

Notice what Isaiah says in the last paragraph of this passage:

In the year that King Uzziah died, I saw the Lord, high and exalted, seated on a throne; and the train of his robe filled the temple. Above him were seraphim, each with six wings: With two wings they covered their faces, with two they covered their feet, and with two they were flying. And they were calling to one another:

> "Holy, holy, holy is the LORD Almighty;
>> the whole earth is full of his glory."

At the sound of their voices the doorposts and thresholds shook and the temple was filled with smoke.

"Woe to me!" I cried. "I am ruined! For I am a man of unclean lips, and I live among a people of unclean lips, and my eyes have seen the King, the LORD Almighty."

Then one of the seraphim flew to me with a live coal in his hand, which he had taken with tongs from the altar. With it he touched my mouth and said, "See, this has touched your lips; your guilt is taken away and your sin atoned for."

(Isaiah 6:1–7)

Why would a live coal from the altar be a good symbol for taking away the guilt of Isaiah's mouth?

If your list of ten items didn't show that you are struggling with a temper, what did it show? For example, does thinking about saying edifying things help you increase the number of things you say to build others up? Or do you nag people who respond by tuning you out?

What if we made an effort to speak the good stuff instead of always picking out the bad? What if I said, "I love you so much! You did a really good job today with your homework. I'm proud of what you did on this test. I know you studied hard. I love watching you play soccer. You did such a good job"?

—*Melanie*

Who can you build up through your words to them?

What might you say to them?

The truth is that we have a God who says we are so much more than that. How different would our lives be if we said, "I'm a child of God, so I'm found and I'm yours and I'm whole and I'm made pure." So, it's out of that overflow in our hearts that we can pour that into somebody else who's in our lives.

—*Melanie*

Think about being whole and pure and found and belonging to God. Then put something inside the following picture frame that expresses your heart on this truth. Write a paragraph or a single phrase, draw a picture or paste a photo, record a line from a favorite song or poem.

Listen to the Word

Take a break from Ruth this week to look at the story of words in the life of the apostle Simon Peter. The first Bible passage below takes place at the last meal Jesus and his followers had together before his arrest and execution. The second passage tells what Peter did just a few hours later, when Jesus had just been arrested. The third passage depicts Jesus and Peter at a breakfast sometime after Jesus rose from the dead.

[Jesus said] "Simon, Simon, Satan has asked to sift all of you as wheat. But I have prayed for you, Simon, that your faith may not fail. And when you have turned back, strengthen your brothers."

But [Peter] replied, "Lord, I am ready to go with you to prison and to death."

Jesus answered, "I tell you, Peter, before the rooster crows today, you will deny three times that you know me."

(Luke 22:31–34)

Then seizing [Jesus], they led him away and took him into the house of the high priest. Peter followed at a distance. And when some there had kindled a fire in the middle of the courtyard and had sat down together, Peter sat down with them. A servant girl saw him seated there in the firelight. She looked closely at him and said, "This man was with him."

But he denied it. "Woman, I don't know him," he said.

A little later someone else saw him and said, "You also are one of them."

"Man, I am not!" Peter replied.

About an hour later another asserted, "Certainly this fellow was with him, for he is a Galilean."

Peter replied, "Man, I don't know what you're talking about!" Just as he was speaking, the rooster crowed. The Lord turned and looked straight at Peter. Then Peter remembered the word the Lord had spoken to him: "Before the rooster crows today, you will disown me three times." And he went outside and wept bitterly.

(Luke 22:54–62)

When they had finished eating, Jesus said to Simon Peter, "Simon son of John, do you love me more than these?"

"Yes, Lord," he said, "you know that I love you."

Jesus said, "Feed my lambs."

Again Jesus said, "Simon son of John, do you love me?"

He answered, "Yes, Lord, you know that I love you."

Jesus said, "Take care of my sheep."

The third time he said to him, "Simon son of John, do you love me?"

Peter was hurt because Jesus asked him the third time, "Do you love me?" He said, "Lord, you know all things; you know that I love you."

Jesus said, "Feed my sheep. Very truly I tell you, when you were younger you dressed yourself and went where you wanted; but when you are old you will stretch out your hands, and someone else will dress you and lead you where you do not want to go." Jesus said this to indicate the kind of death by which Peter would glorify God. Then he said to him, "Follow me!"

(John 21:15–19)

In the first passage above, what do Peter's words reveal about his heart—his self-image, his beliefs, his emotions?

He didn't say anything in response to Jesus' prediction, but what do you think he was thinking about the prediction?

In the second passage, what do Peter's words reveal about his heart? What was he feeling and believing?

What did he feel and believe after the cock crowed? How do we know?

In the third passage, how did Jesus use words wisely to give Peter a chance to restore their relationship? Why do you think he didn't just say something straightforward like, "Peter, you disowned me three times, but I forgive you"?

What do you learn from Jesus' words and Peter's words in these passages about the power of words for good and for ill? How are their words relevant to your own words?

Respond to God

Try to pay attention to your words this week. If you catch yourself saying something you wish you hadn't, send up a quick prayer of apology to God, and also apologize to the person to whom you misspoke. If you get a chance to build someone up with your words, seize it! If you miss the chance, tell God what you wish you'd said. If you like, you can rehearse ahead of time using the letter on the next page. There's no shame in planning your words ahead of time.

What I will say to God if I say something I shouldn't:

What I will say to the other person:

Something upbuilding I can say to (name them):

Something upbuilding I can say to (name them):

What I want to say to God about my words right now:

Session Four

Broken Pieces

The Lord is close to the brokenhearted
and saves those who are crushed in spirit.

Psalm 34:18

Getting Settled

The following paragraphs will orient you to what's coming in this session. Have a group member read them aloud.

Vintage. Distressed. These are fancy, fashionable words for old and recycled. So fashionable, in fact, that you can go on Pinterest to learn how to distress brand new wood so that it looks like it came from a hundred-year-old barn. It's a lot of work, but worth it if you're into shabby chic.

Somehow, though, we haven't made the leap to being comfortable with ourselves as vintage and distressed. We want our bodies to look young and our souls to be as unscarred as fresh laminate flooring.

Unfortunately, most of us have chips and cracks in our souls from the things others have done to us and the poor decisions we ourselves have made along the way. And we often make the mistake of thinking that God expects us to buff out those marks on our own.

> Sometimes we make it really complicated, like there's all these steps that we need to do, or these broken pieces of our lives that we don't feel like Jesus can redeem, or that we can't bring to him. But I think that's why he always seeks us out, no matter how lost or broken we may be, no matter how far we've run, no matter how much we've tried to escape him; he always comes back to us and he finds us wherever we are, wherever our well is at noon, where we feel shunned and lost and broken, and he finds us there because he loves us and because he doesn't want us to stay broken.
>
> —Melanie

In this session, we're going to connect our stories to the story of a broken woman Jesus pursued and won for himself. We'll see that these scars we carry, that seem so big and disqualifying to us, are actually small things he wants to gather up into his healing arms.

Checking In

Give each group member up to two minutes to share answers to these questions. Your group leader can go first.

What is one thing you learned or gained from the On Your Own exercises this past week?

When you were a child, what did you usually do when you were hurt or when something broke?

Video Notes

Watch the video teaching segment for session 4. Use the outline below to fill in your thoughts about what you get out of the video.

Woman at the well

Breaking engagement

Five husbands

Jesus is the only thing that will fill us up.

Telling others

Breakaway Bible study

Kicking It Around

Discuss the following questions in your group. If there are more than twelve of you, consider dividing into smaller groups for discussion. Or select those questions that seem most compelling to you.

1. Which of Melanie's thoughts from this session's video resonated most with you, and why?

2. In your experience or as you have observed other people, how does Jesus go about seeking out broken people and drawing them close for healing?

3. What is our role in Jesus's ministry of healing people's broken pieces?

Jacob's well was there [in the town of Sychar in Samaria], and Jesus, tired as he was from the journey, sat down by the well. It was about noon.

When a Samaritan woman came to draw water, Jesus said to her, "Will you give me a drink?" (His disciples had gone into the town to buy food.)

The Samaritan woman said to him, "You are a Jew and I am a Samaritan woman. How can you ask me for a drink?" (For Jews do not associate with Samaritans.)

Jesus answered her, "If you knew the gift of God and who it is that asks you for a drink, you would have asked him and he would have given you living water."

"Sir," the woman said, "you have nothing to draw with and the well is deep. Where can you get this living water? Are you greater than our father Jacob, who gave us the well and drank from it himself, as did also his sons and his livestock?"

Jesus answered, "Everyone who drinks this water will be thirsty again, but whoever drinks the water I give them will never thirst. Indeed, the water I give them will become in them a spring of water welling up to eternal life."

The woman said to him, "Sir, give me this water so that I won't get thirsty and have to keep coming here to draw water."

He told her, "Go, call your husband and come back."

"I have no husband," she replied.

Jesus said to her, "You are right when you say you have no husband. The fact is, you have had five husbands, and the man you now have is not your husband. What you have just said is quite true."

"Sir," the woman said, "I can see that you are a prophet. Our ancestors worshiped on this mountain, but you Jews claim that the place where we must worship is in Jerusalem."

"Woman," Jesus replied, "believe me, a time is coming when you will worship the Father neither on this mountain nor in Jerusalem. You Samaritans worship what you do not know; we worship what we do know, for salvation is from the Jews. Yet a time is coming and has now come when the true worshipers will worship the Father in the Spirit and in truth, for they are the kind of worshipers the Father seeks. God is spirit, and his worshipers must worship in the Spirit and in truth."

The woman said, "I know that Messiah" (called Christ) "is coming. When he comes, he will explain everything to us."

Then Jesus declared, "I, the one speaking to you—I am he."

(John 4:6–26)

---

4. What goes on in your mind and heart when Jesus says to you, "I, the one speaking to you—I am he"? What do you want to do or say in response?

5. What is something broken in your life that Jesus has healed?

She feels all of a sudden she's so vulnerable and she's so exposed. And that's what it's like when all of a sudden Jesus comes face to face and confronts us with our brokenness. It feels awkward and painful, and what do we do with it? Am I going to trust you and let you come in and heal those broken places in me, or am I going to hold them close and continue to live in my hurt and my brokenness?

—Melanie

6. What would make your group a safe place for you to admit to having something broken in your life that needs restoration from Jesus?

Jesus is the only thing that really fills us up. We go through life and we try to find all these things that we think are going to be the thing that fills us. Maybe when we get a certain degree of education, when we get a certain job, when we have a certain amount of kids, when our kids achieve this thing, when we get this promotion, when we get married, whatever that thing is, and we're just waiting for all these things that we think are going to fill us. And then there we are in our brokenness looking for that thing and Jesus shows up and we say, "What is it?" And he says, "I am him. Guess what, I'm the Messiah, I can give you living water, you'll never be thirsty again." In that moment, if we'll accept it, if we'll really take that in, he can heal whatever is broken in us and we can realize we are never too far gone for him, and he wants to meet us where we are.

—*Melanie*

7. What are the things you've tried (currently or in the past) to fill your life with other than Jesus? What were or are the results?

8. Is there an area of brokenness in your life that you would like the group to pray for? If so, please share it.

Trying It Out

The group leader will need to plan ahead of time to bring blank paper and pens for this exercise. Give everyone a blank sheet of paper and a pen.

Take a few minutes on your own to write down one area of brokenness in your life that you need Jesus to redeem, or one area that he has already redeemed that you are grateful for. Nobody will see this if you don't want them to.

Now write the name of someone to whom you could safely share this information. The route to healing lies through allowing the people of God to be his presence in your life. Or if you have written about something that has already been healed, that's worth celebrating with someone else.

If you can't think of anyone with whom you can safely share, ask God to bring someone trustworthy into your life. You desperately need a friend.

Keep your piece of paper. You will return to it in the On Your Own work during the week.

On Your Own

Session Four

If you really want to get somewhere in this study, take some time before the next group session to work through these solo exercises.

Listen to Your Life

Reread the sheet of paper from the group meeting on which you wrote about your experience of brokenness. Then pray, contact the person whose name you wrote down, and make a coffee date with that person to talk about your experience of brokenness and where you are now with it. If the other person can't meet with you for several weeks, that's okay. The goal here is to begin opening up to someone about your experience and to ask this person to pray for you.

What if you don't have a close friend with whom you normally share confidences? As we'll discuss in session 5, you need at least one or two people in your life like that. It's a priority. You won't heal if nobody knows you. Choose someone in your small group, and ask her if she has twenty minutes to hear your story and pray for you. Don't listen to the voices of shame that would keep you from reaching out.

Or choose someone you know from your church. Feel free to say, "I'm in a Bible study, and they asked us to be open with someone about an area of brokenness in our lives, and I wonder if you have twenty minutes sometime to hear a piece of my story. I think of you as someone who prays for others, and I'm hoping you will pray for me." Ask God for discernment and timing.

If what you wrote down was a past experience of brokenness and healing that you want to celebrate, consider sharing it with someone who isn't a churchgoing Christian.

Choose someone for whom the idea of brokenness won't be an alien concept. Someone who is heavily invested in appearing to have life all together may not be receptive, but someone who has been through a divorce or who shows signs of struggling in her life might be grateful to have an overture of vulnerability from you. Again, you could say something like, "I'm in a study group, and they have urged us to tell someone about something we've been through in our lives, and I thought of you because you seem like a receptive person. I only need ten minutes if you're busy."

Remember that you are sharing this story not to make yourself look good but to make God seem intriguing to the person you're talking to and to be helpful to that person. If you are only acquaintances, and you feel it would be inappropriate to just dive into a highly personal story, you can begin with a coffee date where you spend most of your time getting to know this person. You can then judge whether sharing a piece of your story will be appropriate to this meeting, or whether you will need to save it for a future time. Pray for guidance.

Either way, think ahead of time about how you might keep your story brief and to the point. If you tend to be talkative, consider writing your story down and keeping it under seven hundred words. That's about five minutes. If you're nervous about opening up to someone who might not be a close friend who knows your secrets already, consider what Melanie said in the video:

> Don't we get afraid that there are going to be eye rolls and people are going to be like, "I know you. I know who you are. I know how broken you are. I know you've had five husbands." But [the Samaritan woman] didn't care. Because that's what Jesus does when we begin to see ourselves in his eyes and the way he heals us and the way he uses the broken pieces of our lives. He makes us whole, and what we want to do is use that to make a difference in our world.
>
> —*Melanie*

Another thing you can do if you have an ongoing area of brokenness in your life is to go to Jesus about it on your own. Write out a prayer to Jesus (see next page) asking him to help you with this area and guide you to other resources to help you. Tell him all about your situation—even though he knows it already, it will help you if you put words to your experience.

Dear Jesus,

My situation is this:

What I think I need from you is:

I'm wondering if you think I should do this:

Thank you! I love you!

If praying gives you an insight into what you can do to take a step forward, be sure to take that step as well.

If you don't know what you're doing, pray to the Father. He loves to help. You'll get his help, and won't be condescended to when you ask for it. Ask boldly, believingly, without a second thought. People who "worry their prayers" are like wind-whipped waves. Don't think you're going to get anything from the Master that way, adrift at sea, keeping all your options open.

(James 1:5–8 MSG)

Listen to the Word

We're returning to the book of Ruth this week. Remember that a "guardian-redeemer" (see Ruth 3:9, 12, 13) is a relative willing to take responsibility for restoring a person's rights. In this chapter, Ruth asks Boaz to marry her (and, as we later learn, to buy her late husband's property) to keep both widow and property in the family. Boaz is not legally required to marry his kinsman's widow, but to do so would show family loyalty.

The threshing floor is an open area, often on top of a hill, where there is usually a good breeze in the evening. The workers use winnowing fans to toss piles of barley into the air, and the breeze blows away the chaff while the heavier grain falls to the ground. Boaz is spending the night at the threshing floor to guard against the theft of his grain.

Read Ruth 3.

What do you learn about Ruth from her actions in this chapter? For example:

• What could go wrong with her plan? What could that cost her?

- Why is she going after Boaz rather than a younger man?

- A widow is considered a broken person in ancient Israel. She owns nothing and has an extremely low status. How is Ruth dealing with her brokenness?

What do you learn about Boaz from his actions in this chapter? For example:

- How could he take advantage of Ruth?

- What will it cost him to go along with her plan?

- Why does he care about this broken widow from a foreign country?

Where is God in this part of the story?

What in this chapter of Ruth is relevant to you as you seek to discern God in the small things and in the broken areas of your life?

Respond to God

What is going through your mind right now regarding your past or present brokenness? Are there some lines of a favorite song coming to you? Do you want to draw a picture or print and paste a photo? Are you thinking in phrases or whole sentences? What colors express where you are right now with regard to your brokenness?

Session Five

Investing in Friendships

Your friendship was a miracle-wonder,
      love far exceeding anything I've known—
      or ever hope to know.

2 Samuel 1:26 MSG

Getting Settled

The following paragraphs will orient you to what's coming in this session. Have a group member read them aloud.

In his book *Making Friends (and Making Them Count)*, Em Griffin includes a cartoon showing a man seated behind a desk and a man seated in front of the desk. The man behind the desk sits with relaxed self-confidence and says, "It's not really all that important that we understand each other . . . just that *you* understand *me*."[2]

Some people go into most relationships like that, demanding to be understood but not caring to understand the other. They may have spouses, children, colleagues, employees, and acquaintances, but what they don't have is friends, because friendship requires mutual effort to understand each other. Friendship also requires trust, accountability, transparency, listening, forgiveness, and many other qualities that would make it seem like hard work if it didn't pay such rich dividends.

> We need time with those people who will listen to our stories, and be there for us as we go through heartbreak and joy, and figure out all that life throws our way. Loyal soldiers who will defend us and stand with us when times get hard and when it feels like the world is against us. We need to spend time with our people.
>
> —Melanie

In this session, we will consider why friendship is worth the investment of time and energy, and we'll aim to take some steps toward deepening our friendships.

Checking In

Give each group member up to two minutes to share answers to these questions. Your group leader can go first.

What is one thing you learned or gained from the On Your Own exercises this past week?

What do you most like to do with your friends?

Video Notes

Watch the video teaching segment for session 5. Use the outline below to fill in your thoughts about what you get out of the video.

The importance of deep friendships

God puts specific people in our path.

What do you have that you can offer your friends?

Never underestimate the importance of loyalty.

There's no room for comparison or jealousy.

Our true friends strengthen our grip on God.

Kicking It Around

Discuss the following questions in your group. If there are more than twelve of you, consider dividing into smaller groups for discussion. Or select those questions that seem most compelling to you.

1. Which of Melanie's thoughts from this session's video resonated most with you, and why?

2. What qualities do you look for in a friend?

3. Do you have enough close friends? What makes you answer the way you did?

Our girlfriends are these small pieces of our lives. They're this luminous thread that weaves the woman that we were before we were a wife and mom to the woman that we are now and that we're trying to be to the woman that God has for us to be. And so, I think that it's so important that we invest in those friendships and those relationships. Studies actually show it produces serotonin in our brains that helps ease feelings of depression and stress. It helps us to have people that we can relate to and help us to feel normal.

— Melanie

4. What helps you make time for friends? Or what gets in the way? What can you do about the things that get in the way?

After David had finished talking with Saul, Jonathan became one in spirit with David, and he loved him as himself. From that day Saul kept David with him and did not let him return home to his family. And Jonathan made a covenant with David because he loved him as himself. Jonathan took off the robe he was wearing and gave it to David, along with his tunic, and even his sword, his bow and his belt.

(1 Samuel 18:1–4)

---

5. David was perhaps sixteen years old when the above passage took place. Jonathan was several years older, and a king's son, so he had fine clothes and weapons. A "covenant" was an agreement about mutual responsibilities and brotherly bond of commitment. Today we don't usually formalize friendship with stated covenants. Instead, we have unspoken expectations about what each person will do and not do. What are some of the things you would like a friend to do?

What are some things you expect a friend not to do? Why?

We all have our own gifts and our own things and our own paths that we're called to walk. And I know for me I never get more distracted than when I start looking at somebody else's life and what they're doing. Nothing will get me off my game more than when I go to Pinterest and I can see some mom who's made those cookies that look like a melting snowman, and I'm like "I'm the lamest mom ever," because not only do I not know how to make those cookies, I don't want to *learn* how to make those cookies.

—*Melanie*

6. What's wrong with comparing ourselves to other people?

7. What for you is the most challenging part of friendship? What is the area where you most need help from God?

Trying It Out

Pair up with a partner. Take ten minutes just to get to know each other better. Try to make the listening and the talking roughly even between you. See if you can discern the right level of personal disclosure based on how well you already know each other. What questions can you ask each other to get the ball rolling at a level that is more than just superficial? For example:

- What was the most challenging part of your week this week?
- What was the best part of your week?
- Are you more comfortable being a talker or a listener? Why is that the case?
- How can I pray for you this week?

On Your Own

Session Five

If you really want to get somewhere in this study, take some time before the next group session to work through these solo exercises.

Listen to Your Life

What do you have that you can offer your friends? Do you have time? Do you have re-sources? Do you have talents? Can you sit with them at the hospital? Can you take their kids to school? Can you show up with a meal on a day when you know they've had a hard week?

—Melanie

Part One

What do you have that you can offer your friends? Make a list of your inner qualities and practical resources. If you have trouble identifying at least ten things, tell your inner critic to take a hike. You have more to offer than you give yourself credit for.

1. _____
2. _____
3. _____

4. _____

5. _____

6. _____

7. _____

8. _____

9. _____

10. _____

Write down the names of your close friends. These people are more than acquaintances, more than social media friends. These are the people with whom you actually share life. There's no rule about how many friends a person should have. Some of us flourish with one or two really close friends, while others need a circle of ten.

Thank God for the people you have named. Now write down one thing you could do for each of these people to build them up.

Make plans to get together with at least one friend. Don't have time? What can you do about that? Pray for help.

Part Two

Maybe you've tried to list your close friends or tried to make plans with a friend and you've found that you don't have anybody close enough to just call and make plans with. Or you have loads of people to hang out with, but no one whom you allow to really know you. There's no one with whom you share that mutual trust that your soul needs. What can you do about that?

Write down the name of one person with whom you would like to deepen a friendship. Maybe you're acquaintances, but you see in her the potential for more. Try not to name the busiest and most popular person you know. (No, we never quite escape junior high.)

_____

Now pray for this person and for your relationship with her. Ask God to bless her in all her areas of joy and sadness and hope and frustration. Ask God to show you what you can do to build her up. See if you can write down one thing you can do.

Part Three

Maybe you're reluctant to get close to anyone because you've been burned by a friend in the past.

This isn't the neighborhood bully
    mocking me—I could take that.
This isn't a foreign devil spitting
    invective—I could tune that out.
It's *you*! We grew up together!
    You! My best friend!
Those long hours of leisure as we walked
    arm in arm, God a third party to our conversation.

(Psalm 55:12–14 MSG)

If you've been burned, write about your experience, or draw a picture that portrays that experience and how you feel about it. Or just splash phrases and sketches on the page. Get it all out.

Are you going to let past hurts keep you from present and future flourishing? Explain why you are or aren't.

[Our daughter] Caroline . . . had to write a book of five poems for her seventh-grade English final, and as I was reading through her words, I was struck by one line in particular: "some people stand out more than others, like neon posters on a beige wall."

I wondered if she sees herself as the beige wall or the neon poster, because she is nothing if not a neon poster kind of girl. But the junior high years can cause you to question everything from the way you look to what you believe as you and your friends grow and change at such a rapid pace.

The following weekend, I was at the pool with Caroline and one of her best friends, Maddy. As I watched the two of them jump off the edge of the pool and laugh until they cried and talk endlessly as they baked in the sun, it dawned on me that this kind of friendship is what helps you be a neon poster. It's the knowledge that you have people who know you and love you and encourage you, that help you be the best and brightest version of yourself. So I thought it was fitting that Caroline ended her poem with a line about how sometimes you may not notice the beige wall, but it is the thing that holds up the neon poster. The beige wall allows the neon poster to shine bright.

One of the reasons I'm so fascinated by having a daughter who falls closer to the neon poster end of the spectrum is because I spent years seeing myself as more of a beige wall. It's true. I wanted to be the girl who dances without feeling self-conscious or tells the funny stories that make everyone laugh and believe the party wouldn't be half as much fun without you. But as I've gotten older, I've realized the truth is that we should all have a little bit of neon poster and a little bit of beige wall in ourselves.

Sometimes our role is to be brighter than the sun, and sometimes our role is to sit back and cheer on our friends as their gifts are on display. My friend Jamie's mom once told her, "Every relationship has a peacock and a grouse." I think that's true. When I look at my closest friends, I can totally see a pattern. I am drawn to peacocks. I love being surrounded by funny, witty, bright, strong-willed women who aren't afraid to take charge of almost any situation. I tend to approach social situations—and life—a little more cautiously, and the friends I have chosen along the way have taught me the joy of jumping in with both feet, embracing a challenge, and not being afraid to love with your whole heart. We all love each other fiercely. They are my cheerleaders, my first call, my sanity, and a big chunk of my heart.

—Church of the Small Things, pages 194–196

Listen to the Word

Read the following proverbs, and for each one write down how it is telling you to live.

The righteous choose their friends carefully,
    but the way of the wicked leads them astray.

(Proverbs 12:26)

The person who shuns the bitter moments of friends
    will be an outsider at their celebrations.

(Proverbs 14:10 MSG)

Overlook an offense and bond a friendship;
    fasten on to a slight and—good-bye, friend!

(Proverbs 17:9 MSG)

A friend loves at all times,
    and a brother is born for a time of adversity.

(Proverbs 17:17)

Do a favor and win a friend forever;
    nothing can untie that bond.

(Proverbs 18:19 MSG)

Friends come and friends go,
    but a true friend sticks by you like family.

                                          (Proverbs 18:24 MSG)

Do not make friends with a hot-tempered person,
    do not associate with one easily angered.

                                          (Proverbs 22:24)

The right word at the right time
    is like a custom-made piece of jewelry
And a wise friend's timely reprimand
    is like a gold ring slipped on your finger.

                                          (Proverbs 25:11–12 MSG)

Reliable friends who do what they say
    are like cool drinks in sweltering heat—refreshing!

                                          (Proverbs 25:13 MSG)

Like a cool drink of water when you're worn out and weary
    is a letter from a long-lost friend.

                                          (Proverbs 25:25 MSG)

(cont.)

Wounds from a friend can be trusted,
 but an enemy multiplies kisses.

             (Proverbs 27:6)

Perfume and incense bring joy to the heart,
 and the pleasantness of a friend springs from their heartfelt advice.

             (Proverbs 27:9)

You use steel to sharpen steel,
 and one friend sharpens another.

            (Proverbs 27:17 MSG)

By yourself you're unprotected.
 With a friend you can face the worst.
Can you round up a third?
 A three-stranded rope isn't easily snapped.

           (Ecclesiastes 4:12 MSG)

What do you think Proverbs 27:6 means when it says wounds from a friend can be trusted? How can you know that this isn't a friend stabbing you in the back?

How does one friend sharpen another (Proverbs 27:17)? What does that image mean?

Why do you suppose there are so many proverbs about friendship?

Reread what you wrote about the proverbs. What are the top two or three things about being a friend or choosing a friend that you want to take to heart?

Respond to God

If friendship is a great blessing to you, write a letter to God thanking him for the friends in your life.

If making friends is hard for you, take some time to take this challenge to God. Pray passionately for a true friend. Let your emotions out. Tell God about the times when you've reached out to someone who didn't respond with equal interest. If you have fears of being betrayed or rejected, tell him about your fear. Tell him about your busyness. If you look around you and don't see anyone whom you think would be a great connection for you, ask him to put someone into your life who is the type of person you're drawn to. Ask him to open your eyes to the compatible people in your world.

Dear God,

Much love,

Session Six

Bigger than You Imagine

And we know that in all things God works for the good of those who love him, who have been called according to his purpose.

Romans 8:28

Getting Settled

The following paragraphs will orient you to what's coming in this session. Have a group member read them aloud.

In 1793, George Washington quoted what he said was an old Scottish proverb, "Many mickles make a muckle." What he meant was, many small things add up to something big. The only trouble was that the proverb had "the almost fatal flaw of failure to make sense."[3] That's because "mickle" in the Scottish dialect meant a big thing and "muckle" was just the way some Scottish people pronounced the same word. So Washington was really saying, "Many big things add up to something big." The brave and wise father of our country got it wrong. Oops.

I hope that makes you feel a little better about the times when you get it way wrong. I know I feel better. And the fact is that what Washington meant to say was so true. Many small things do add up to a big thing, a big life. In this final session, we're going to look at some reasons why so many of us doubt this fact and some Scriptures that I hope will ground us in this important truth.

Deep down, we struggle to believe God is going to lead us to what is best for us. It's our internal voice that whispers we will never be enough, so we work and worry and feel like we must do something big, something huge to prove our worth and to make sure our life matters. We have to host a conference, start a movement, adopt fifteen kids, or fight human trafficking to really matter. Which are all great things, but can cause us to lose sight of the small things that can also change a life: bringing dinner to a sick neighbor, smiling at a waitress who's having a bad day, reading to your kids before bed, and simply praying for someone going through a rough time.

—Church of the Small Things, page 215

Checking In

Give each group member up to two minutes to share answers to these questions. Your group leader can go first.

What is one thing you learned or gained from the On Your Own exercises this past week?

How much time per day or per week do you spend on social media or playing games or shopping on a device?

Video Notes

Watch the video teaching segment for session 6. Use the outline below to fill in your thoughts about what you get out of the video.

A generation expected to do it all

Do we believe we have everything we need in Jesus?

Asking why versus asking where

Measuring

Church of the small things

Kicking It Around

Discuss the following questions in your group. If there are more than twelve of you, consider dividing into smaller groups for discussion. Or select those questions that seem most compelling to you.

1. Which of Melanie's thoughts from this session's video resonated most with you, and why?

> We worry and we worry and we worry instead of saying, "God I take you at your word that you've promised to give me all that I need, and that everything I need to be I have in you. And so, I'm going to trust that you mean it. You take all these small pieces of our lives and work them all out together, and you're constantly working all things for our good. And what's at the bottom of our discontentment is our failure to believe that everything we have, everything we need, everything that we're supposed to achieve in life we already have in the person of Jesus Christ.
>
> —Melanie

2. What does it mean to say that everything we need and everything we're supposed to achieve we already have in the person of Jesus Christ? Give some examples.

3. What are the experiences that tempt you to doubt that God is working all things together for your good?

You're asking [God] the wrong question. You're asking why and what you ought to be asking is where. Where do I [God] want you to go? Where do I have plans for you? Where can I use you effectively? Where can you work in your neighborhood and in your community and in your life and in your marriage and in your family to be the person that I designed you to be? Because the why takes on this mentality that there's something better, but the where just says, "God, I'm here, and I want you to use every little piece of my life for your glory."

—*Melanie*

4. Where can God use you effectively?

I looked up, and there before me was a man with a measuring line in his hand. I asked, "Where are you going?"

He answered me, "To measure Jerusalem, to find out how wide and how long it is."

While the angel who was speaking to me was leaving, another angel came to meet him and said to him: "Run, tell that young man, 'Jerusalem will be a city without walls because of the great number of people and animals in it. And I myself will be a wall of fire around it,' declares the LORD, 'and I will be its glory within.'"

(Zechariah 2:1–5)

5. What's wrong with measuring ourselves by what we see in other people and the things they post on social media?

If this is such a big mistake, why do you think we so often do it?

6. What would you say to other people if you let down your walls and were vulnerable?

7. What are the main things you will take away from this study of the *Church of the Small Things?*

Trying It Out

Gather in subgroups of three people. Let each person answer the question, "How can we pray for you?" Then pray for each person in your group, asking God to work all things together for her good, even the things that aren't going the way she wishes they would go. Pray that Jesus would hold together all the small things in her life. Pray that he would make her city bigger than she can imagine.

On Your Own

Session Six

If you really want to get somewhere in this study, take some time in the coming days to work through these solo exercises.

Listen to Your Life

As you did in sessions 1 and 2, write down ten things you've done this week to make someone else's life better.

1. _____
2. _____
3. _____
4. _____
5. _____
6. _____
7. _____
8. _____

9. _____

10. _____

Do you notice any changes since you made your list in session 1? (See page 19.) For example, do you have more joy, or a sense of meaning and purpose, in doing these small things? Are you pushing yourself outside your comfort zone more often? Write down anything you notice.

What is one small thing you could do for someone else this week that is outside your normal routine?

Sometimes I think what God is saying is, "You know where I want to use you: in your cubicle at work, with those students that come into your classroom every day, making pies in the restaurant that your family started all those years ago. That's where your ministry is. That's exactly where I placed you because I knew that you were uniquely designed for this time and this generation and this purpose. And there's this small corner of the world that isn't going to look the way it's supposed to look if you're not dialing into . . . all the plans and purposes I have for you there. There's also being kind to your neighbor, reaching out to somebody who's hurt, delivering a meal to somebody you know who's sick.

— *Melanie*

Describe the small corner of the world where God has plans and purposes for you.

How content are you to serve there? Do you still feel like you're not enough if that's your whole world for now?

For in him all things were created: things in heaven and on earth, visible and invisible, whether thrones or powers or rulers or authorities; all things have been created through him and for him. He is before all things, and in him all things hold together. And he is the head of the body, the church; he is the beginning and the firstborn from among the dead, so that in everything he might have the supremacy.

(Colossians 1:16–18)

Go out and buy or gather something that will remind you to value the small things in your life. For instance, go to a craft store and get a bowlful of small polished stones. Or buy a necklace of many tiny beads. Wear your beads, or put your bowl of stones someplace where you will see it often and be reminded. Each time you see your memento, take a moment to thank God for one small thing in your life. Develop this as a habit that you can carry with you through the ups and downs of your life.

There are all these small pieces of our lives. There are all these small things that may seem insignificant to us. But Jesus is over all of them. They were created for him and by him. And he works through us to create purposes and plans that we couldn't imagine on our own.

—Melanie

Draw a picture that represents your life with all of the small things that make it up.

Not all of us can do great things. But we can do small things with great love.

—Teresa of Calcutta

Listen to the Word

At last we're going to finish the story of Ruth. The final chapter is largely taken up with a legal transaction. Clans were very important in ancient Israel, and land was supposed to stay in the clan, even when a man died without heirs. It was considered a great tragedy for a person to die without heirs, and Ruth was showing loyalty to her late husband's family by marrying one of his relatives, so that his name wouldn't die out in the family. Ruth's firstborn son would be considered the heir of Mahlon and the grandson of Naomi. This child would also inherit the land Naomi was selling.

Read Ruth 4.

What are the big moments in this chapter?

How are these big moments dependent on small things that led up to them?

What small things would the birth of Obed oblige Ruth to do?

Why do you think the author of Ruth gives us the genealogy of David at the end of this story?

Taken altogether, how does the book of Ruth illustrate the themes of the *Church of the Small Things?*

What will you take away from the book of Ruth that is relevant to your life?

Respond to God

When you start asking God, "Where do you want me, and where can you use all these small pieces of my life and all this stuff that I do?" God is going to make that city so large that walls can't contain it.

—Melanie

Write a letter to God, telling him what you've gotten out of this study of the *Church of the Small Things.*

Dear God,

Thank you so much for

Some of the things I've learned that I don't want to forget are

What I long for you to do in my life is

Please help me with

Much love,

Notes

1. Gordon MacDonald, "God's Calling Plan," *CTpastors*, Fall 2003, http://www .christianitytoday.com/pastors/2003/fall/3.35.html.
2. Cartoon from *The Wall Street Journal*. Permission from Cartoon Features Syndicate, as depicted in Em Griffin, *Making Friends (and Making Them Count)* (Downers Grove, IL: InterVarsity Press, 1987), 23.
3. Bartlett Jere Whiting, *Early American Proverbs and Proverbial Phrases*, quoted in James Breig, "Puttin' on the Dog: Adventures in the Idioms of Our Mother Tongue," *Colonial Williamsburg Journal*, Summer 2002, https://www.history.org/ Foundation/journal/Summer02/puttin_on_the_dog.cfm.

Church of the Small Things

The Million Little Pieces That Make Up a Life

Melanie Shankle

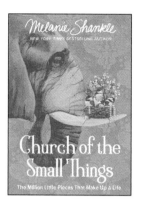

Is my ordinary, everyday life actually significant? Is it okay to be fulfilled by the simple acts of raising kids, working in an office, and cooking chicken for dinner?

It's been said, "Life is not measured by the number of breaths we take, but by the number of moments that take our breath away." The pressure of that can be staggering as we spend our days looking for that big thing that promises to take our breath away. Meanwhile, we lose sight of the small significance of fully living with every breath we take.

Melanie Shankle, *New York Times* bestselling author and writer at *The Big Mama Blog* tackles these questions head on in her fourth book, *Church of the Small Things*. Easygoing and relatable, she speaks directly to the heart of women of all ages who are longing to find significance and meaning in the normal, sometimes mundane world of driving carpool to soccer practice, attending class on their college campus, cooking meals for their family, or taking care of a sick loved one.

The million little pieces that make a life aren't necessarily glamorous or far-reaching. But God uses some of the smallest, most ordinary acts of faithfulness—and sometimes they look a whole lot like packing lunch.

Through humorous stories told in her signature style, full of Frito pie, best friends, the love of her Me-Ma and Pa-Pa, the unexpected grace that comes when we quit trying to measure up, and a little of the best TV has to offer, Melanie helps women embrace what it means to live a simple, yet incredibly meaningful life and how to find all the beauty and laughter that lies right beneath the surface of every moment.